ANTONY & CLEOPATRA: A GUIDE

The Shakespeare Handbooks

Available now:

- Antony & Cleopatra

- As You Like It

- King Lear

- Twelfth Night

Available Spring 1996:

- Macbeth

- Julius Caesar

Further titles in preparation.

The Shakespeare Handbooks

Antony & Cleopatra

A Guide

by Alistair McCallum

Upstart Crow Publications

First published in 1996 by:

Upstart Crow Publications
11 St John's Terrace
Lewes, East Sussex
BN7 2DL

Copyright © Alistair McCallum 1995

A CIP catalogue record for this book
is available from the British Library

ISBN 1 899747 02 8

Printed in Great Britain by The Book Factory,
35/37 Queensland Road, London N7 7AH

Cover graphic by Hazel Barker

Setting the scene

Shakespeare wrote *Antony and Cleopatra* in or around 1607. He was in his early forties, and was the principal playwright for the King's Men, widely regarded as the best theatre company in London. At this period in his life, Shakespeare was at the peak of his creative powers. In the past few years alone, he had produced the titanic tragic masterpieces of *Othello*, *King Lear* and *Macbeth*.

Antony and Cleopatra is very different in tone from the great tragedies that preceded it. As opposed to their heavy, sometimes bleak vision of humanity, with its terrifying capacity for evil, *Antony and Cleopatra* is marked by lightness, sympathy, balance, and humour. The conflicting worlds of Rome - solid, conformist and disciplined - and Egypt - sultry, luxurious and hedonistic - are presented in a mass of lively, vivid detail, the play swarming with characters, images and movement.

Nothing is known of the first performances of *Antony and Cleopatra*; in fact, the earliest recorded production of the play took place more than a hundred years after Shakespeare's death. A more solemn, sentimental version of the story, *All for Love*, written by Dryden in 1677, was popular for many years, and it was not until the 19th century that *Antony and Cleopatra* was rediscovered as a major work of drama. At this time, lavish productions, with spectacular pageants, sea-battles and marching armies, were favoured.

More recent productions have tried to explore the depth and richness of the text as well as the variety of the action. What strikes us now about *Antony and Cleopatra* is the effortless beauty of its language. Shakespeare was clearly fascinated by the story, which is rendered with considerable historical accuracy, and to see or read the play is to witness one of the world's great poets in his element.

"... over these bare facts Shakespeare throws a great mound of flowers. Never before or afterwards did he lavish the resources of his poetry as he lavishes them here. Page after page of utterly unforgettable verse, perfect in cadence, perfect in metaphor - it is the most dazzling display of the world's most dazzling poet."

John Wain, *The Living World of Shakespeare*, 1964

Rome, 40 B.C.

Julius Caesar has been dead for four years. His death has led to civil war, anarchy and a murderous struggle for power in the vast, ever-expanding Roman Empire.

Caesar's assassins have themselves been killed, and an uneasy peace has finally been established. Three men, each commanding immense resources of wealth, land and arms, have come out on top:

Octavius Caesar	*Antony*	*Lepidus*
Adopted son of Julius Caesar: a strategist: young, determined, self-disciplined.	Previously one of Julius Caesar's generals: a warrior: impulsive, gregarious, generous.	An aristocrat and statesman: mild, peaceable, ineffectual.

These three men - the Triumvirate - now rule the Empire jointly.

Trouble brewing

The civil war, lawlessness and bloodshed have come to a halt for the time being, but the Empire is far from safe. A series of events, both within the Empire and outside it, is threatening its stability:

- Unknown to Antony, **Fulvia**, his wife, has been stirring up rebellion in Rome against Octavius Caesar. Antony's brother is also involved. The two of them have been driven out of Italy, but are still intent on causing trouble.

- At the eastern border of the Empire, in Syria, the Parthians, led by **Labienus**, are making inroads into Roman territory.

- **Sextus Pompeius**, based in Sicily, has taken control of the sea around the south of Italy. He has the support of the mass of disaffected Romans who remember the rule of his father, Pompey the Great, with respect and affection.

Meanwhile, Antony is in Egypt. Infatuated with the Egyptian queen, Cleopatra, he is neglecting the urgent business of the Empire.

Curtain up

Antony puts pleasure before business

In Cleopatra's palace in Alexandria, two of Antony's followers are talking, disapprovingly, of the change that has come over their leader. Since becoming entangled with Cleopatra, they believe, he is no longer the valiant, disciplined warrior that he once was: he has become nothing more than the plaything of the Egyptian queen.

As they talk, Antony and Cleopatra enter, attended by the handmaidens and eunuchs of Cleopatra's court.

A messenger arrives from Antony's co-ruler, Octavius Caesar in Rome. Against Cleopatra's advice, Antony ignores him. He is lost in the immediacy of his own passion, and is only interested in the enjoyment of the moment:

> *Antony:* ... for the love of Love, and her soft hours,
> Let's not confound the time with conference harsh:
> There's not a minute of our lives should stretch
> Without some pleasure now.

Antony's followers watch helplessly as the two lovers and their attendants sweep out again, disregarding Caesar's messenger. He is no longer his own man, they feel; what's more, his reputation has become the subject of gossip and rumour back in Rome.

"Shakespeare divined, long before England became an imperial power, one of the most difficult problems of imperialism: how to stop your personnel from going native."

John Wain, *The Living World of Shakespeare*, 1964

The soothsayer speaks

Charmian and Iras, Cleopatra's attendants - who are also her closest companions and confidantes - have decided to have their fortunes told. The soothsayer is brought in to read their palms.

In contrast to the others, the soothsayer is thoughtful and serious, and his utterances are brief and enigmatic. His first prediction for Charmian is promising:

> *Char.:* Good sir, give me good fortune.
> *Sooth.:* I make not, but foresee.
> *Char.:* Pray then, foresee me one.
> *Sooth.:* You shall be yet far fairer than you are.

He also predicts that she will live longer than Cleopatra. Some of his other comments are more ominous:

> *Sooth.:* You have seen and prov'd a fairer former fortune
> Than that which is to approach.

However, in the noisy banter of the company, his prophecies are treated as nothing more than a bit of fun. Enobarbus, Antony's right-hand man, who has already called out for wine to be provided, makes a more down-to-earth prediction:

> *Eno.:* Mine, and most of our fortunes to-night, shall
> be - drunk to bed.

Antony makes a decision

Antony finally listens to the messenger from Rome. He learns that his wife, Fulvia, has been stirring up a revolt against Caesar in Italy, and that Labienus has occupied a wide area of Roman territory in the eastern part of the Empire.

Antony realises that his obsession with Cleopatra has distracted him from his duty, and left him oblivious of events in the Empire. Although he finds it painful to be reminded of his negligence, he realises that it is necessary for him to hear the truth:

> *Antony:*   O then we bring forth weeds,
> When our quick* minds lie still, and our ills told us
> Is as our earing.**
>
> ** vital, energetic*
> *** ploughing, harrowing*

Suddenly, another messenger arrives with news of Fulvia's death. Antony knows he should be pleased; it is exactly what he wanted, as it means the end of the rebellion in Italy as well as freedom for him to pursue his relationship with Cleopatra. Instead, to his surprise, he feels a deep sense of loss, and the pleasures of his life in Egypt suddenly seem hollow.

Sensing that he is losing control over events, Antony is jolted into making a decision. He resolves to return to Rome immediately.

Enobarbus takes a cynical view

Antony informs Enobarbus that they must prepare to leave at once. Enobarbus predicts, with amusement, what the reaction to the news will be:

Eno.:   Cleopatra catching but the least noise of this, dies
        instantly. I have seen her die twenty times upon far
        poorer moment: I do think there is mettle* in death,
        which commits some loving act upon her, she hath
        such a celerity** in dying.

        * vigour
        ** speed, willingness

When Antony tells him that Fulvia has died, Enobarbus remains unmoved, and continues to tease his master about his love-affair:

Eno.:   When it pleaseth their deities to take the wife of a
          man from him, it shows to man the tailors of the earth...
          this grief is crown'd with consolation, your old smock
          brings forth a new petticoat, and indeed the tears live
          in an onion, that should water this sorrow.
Antony: The business she hath broached in the state
          Cannot endure my absence.
Eno.:   And the business you have broach'd here cannot be
          without you, especially that of Cleopatra's, which
          wholly depends on your abode.

Antony becomes impatient with Enobarbus's flippant comments. There is serious business to attend to in Rome, he explains: Fulvia's rebellion may be over, but the son of Pompey the Great, Sextus Pompeius, is challenging the Triumvirate, and is gathering the support of discontented Roman citizens. It is time for action.

Cleopatra's passion for Antony is as wholehearted as Antony's for her: but, unlike him, she is able to stand back from her emotions, to calculate and manipulate. She already suspects that Antony intends to return to Rome and (she assumes) to his wife, Fulvia.

When Antony comes to break the news to her, she deliberately becomes changeable and difficult, teasing him about Fulvia's control over him, and reminding him of his earlier willingness to stay in Egypt:

> Cleo.:   ... pray you, seek no colour* for your going,
> But bid farewell, and go: when you sued** staying,
> Then was the time for words; no going then;
> Eternity was in our lips, and eyes,
> Bliss in our brows' bent...***
>
> *excuse*
> **were intent on*
> ***arch*

"You may observe that amongst all the great and worthy Persons... there is not One that hath beene transported to the mad degree of Love; which shewes that great Spirits and great Businesse doe keepe out of this weake Passion. You must except, never the lesse, Marcus Antonius the halfe partner of the Empire of Rome."

Francis Bacon, *Of Love*, 1597

Antony tells Cleopatra of the problems in Rome that require his presence. He also tells her of Fulvia's death, a fact which Cleopatra immediately seizes upon to add to his discomfort:

Cleo.:   O most false love!
    Where be the sacred vials thou should'st fill
    With sorrowful water? Now I see, I see,
    In Fulvia's death, how mine receiv'd shall be.

As she continues to tease him, Antony becomes embarrassed and angry. All he can do in his defence is insist, repeatedly, on his faithful, loving devotion to her: and it is on this note of renewed affection that they part.

Meanwhile, back in Rome... I, iv

Octavius Caesar is holding forth to Lepidus on the subject of Antony's faults. Antony's debauchery is bad enough, he says: but his failure to give his support to the Empire, at this time of crisis, is unforgivable. Lepidus attempts to present Antony's negligence in a favourable light, but Caesar has no time for excuses.

Caesar is monitoring the situation in Italy closely, and has ordered a constant flow of information through a network of spies and messengers across the country. One messenger arrives to tell him that Pompey is gaining popular support: he is followed by another who tells him that Pompey has joined forces with two notorious pirates, Menecrates and Menas, and is taking control of the sea around Italy.

The situation in the ports is particularly dangerous, as Pompey's forces are carrying out raids, causing the general population to flee inland:

> *Mess.:*   Many hot inroads
> They make in Italy, the borders maritime
> Lack blood to think on't...
> No vessel can peep forth, but 'tis as soon
> Taken as seen...

The news makes Caesar even more impatient with Antony. He recalls Antony's resilience after the battle of Modena, where Caesar had defeated him, in the days before their partnership. Then, he had endured hunger and cold with fortitude; now, in contrast, he has softened and given himself up to luxury and self-indulgence.

Whatever Antony does, Caesar realises that he and Lepidus must respond to Pompey's threat. The two men set off to prepare their armed forces for action.

A gift for Cleopatra   I, v

Cleopatra is whiling away the time with sleep and languid conversation. Her greatest pleasure is to luxuriate in thoughts and memories of Antony:

> *Cleo.:*   He's speaking now,
> Or murmuring, 'Where's my serpent of old Nile?'
> For so he calls me. Now I feed myself
> With most delicious poison. Think on me,
> That am with Phoebus'* amorous pinches black...
>
> * *the sun god*

She is shaken out of her dreamy state by the arrival of a messenger from Antony. He brings a pearl, and reports Antony's promise that he will make up for his absence with gifts of kingdoms.

Cleopatra, excited to hear from Antony, decides to write him one of her frequent letters. Teased by her attendant Charmian, she insists that in comparison to her love for Antony, her earlier feelings for Julius Caesar - who had been both her lover and political protector - were just youthful infatuation:

Char.:   The valiant Caesar!
Cleo.:   By Isis, I will give thee bloody teeth,
           If thou with Caesar paragon* again
           My man of men.
Char.:   By your most gracious pardon,
           I sing but after you.**
Cleo.:   My salad days,
           When I was green in judgment, cold in blood,
           To say as I said then.

           * compare
           ** I'm only singing his praises as you used to

"*Cleopatra's sense of self is very acute; she is a constant manipulator of illusion and reality, herself the embodiment of the irrational, the ultimate exception to all rules...*"

Marjorie B. Garber, *Dream in Shakespeare: from Metaphor to Metamorphosis*, 1974

Conspiracy in Sicily

Pompey is plotting a full-scale assault on the Empire, with the help of the pirates Menecrates and Menas. He is taken aback to hear that Caesar and Lepidus are mobilising against him; he had been banking on continuing disunity within the Triumvirate.

He consoles himself with the thought that Antony - entangled as he is with Cleopatra in Egypt - does not present a problem. However, this illusion too is shattered when news arrives that Antony is already on his way to Rome. This is a major setback, but Pompey puts a brave face on it:

Pompey: ... I did not think
         This amorous surfeiter* would have donn'd his helm
         For such a petty war: his soldiership
         Is twice the other twain: but let us rear
         The higher our opinion, that our stirring
         Can from the lap of Egypt's widow pluck
         The ne'er-lust-wearied Antony.

         * *over-indulger*

It remains to be seen whether the three leaders can set aside their differences and unite against the planned offensive. Either way, Pompey is convinced that justice, and the gods, are on his side.

... the lap of Egypt's widow...

Technically speaking, Cleopatra was, as Pompey says, a widow. She was the last of the Ptolemies, the dynasty that had ruled Egypt for nearly three centuries, and she had inherited the throne while still in her teens. Incestuous marriages were not unusual among the Ptolemies, and Cleopatra was married to her own brother, who was even younger than her.

A few years after coming to power, Cleopatra was briefly deposed in a coup carried out by her brother's supporters. However, her brother died in suspicious circumstances - almost certainly poisoned by Cleopatra - and she quickly regained the Egyptian throne.

The three rulers have arranged to meet in order to consider the threats facing the Empire.

While waiting for the others to arrive, Lepidus is trying to persuade Enobarbus that this is a time for calmness and diplomacy; personal differences between Caesar and Antony should be set aside. The blunt, belligerent Enobarbus is having none of it:

Lep.:   Good Enobarbus, 'tis a worthy deed,
And shall become you well, to entreat your captain
To soft and gentle speech.

Eno.:   I shall entreat him
To answer like himself: if Caesar move* him,
Let Antony look over Caesar's head,
And speak as loud as Mars...

Lep.:   'Tis not a time
For private stomaching.

Eno.:   Every time
Serves for the matter that is then born in't.

Lep.:   But small to greater matters must give way.
Eno.:   Not if the small come first.

   * *anger*

Antony and Caesar arrive, separately, and conspicuously ignore one another. After a plea for friendship and unity from Lepidus, the two men coolly exchange greetings. Their disagreements immediately come to the surface, and their manner becomes less formal and more heated as the argument proceeds.

Caesar criticises Antony for remaining in Egypt while his wife and brother were causing trouble in Rome, and for ignoring his messenger. Antony jokes and blusters defensively. His wife was beyond any man's control, he claims: and as for Caesar's messenger, Antony had been entertaining three kings the night before his arrival, and hardly knew what time of day it was.

Caesar then comes to a more important point: that Antony had not provided arms and aid when Caesar required them in the fight against Fulvia. This directly contravened the pact of mutual assistance to which all three leaders have solemnly sworn. Antony knows he is in the wrong. Keen to emphasise his honour, he nevertheless gives something approaching an apology:

> *Antony:*   Truth is, that Fulvia,
> To have me out of Egypt, made wars here,
> For which myself, the ignorant motive, do
> So far ask pardon, as befits mine honour
> To stoop in such a case.

It is enough. A temporary unity is established. Lepidus is delighted; Enobarbus remains cynical.

"It is because Antony is so much bigger a man than Caesar that he is also, at other times, so much smaller. Along with Cleopatra, he is often not simply ordinary but silly and childish. Caesar never descends to that level, because he never rises above his own: he has no dreams of divinity..."

Northrop Frye, *On Shakespeare*, 1986

A wedding is announced

Caesar expresses his concern that, whatever agreement he and Antony might come to, it will always be difficult for the two of them to get on together on a personal level.

At this point Agrippa, one of Caesar's advisers, puts forward an idea. He proposes that Antony - a widower now that Fulvia is dead - should marry Caesar's sister Octavia. This, he suggests, will make stable and permanent the goodwill that has now been created between the two men. The idea is seized on enthusiastically by everyone present, and Caesar immediately promises Antony the hand of the absent Octavia.

The three leaders depart together. First, the marriage of Antony to Octavia is to take place: as soon as that is done, the three will deal with the threats facing the Empire. The most urgent is presented by Pompey, who has advanced from his base in Sicily and is now firmly established in Misena, in the south of Italy.

Conspiracy theory: the marriage idea was planned in advance by Caesar, who instructed Agrippa to put forward the suggestion at this conference. The impulsive Antony was sure to accept, but is equally sure to go back to Cleopatra. If he does so, Caesar will be able to take the moral high ground and win the support of all right-minded Romans in any future conflict. In this way, Caesar uses his sister as a pawn in his long-term strategy to defeat Antony.

Tales of Egypt

When the leaders have left, their followers stay behind to chew the fat. Enobarbus is only too ready to confirm his listeners' image of Egypt as a playground of luxury and debauchery.

Then he comes to the subject of Cleopatra, and he reaches soaring heights of poetry as he describes how she first appeared to Antony, in her royal barge, in the burning heat of the day:

> *Eno.:* The barge she sat in, like a burnish'd throne
> Burn'd on the water: the poop was beaten gold;
> Purple the sails, and so perfumed that
> The winds were love-sick with them; the oars were silver,
> Which to the tune of flutes kept stroke, and made
> The water which they beat to follow faster,
> As amorous of their strokes.

Nature itself seemed to be in love with her; and Antony, invited to dine with her, was immediately captivated.

Agrippa recalls that Julius Caesar too had been charmed by the Egyptian queen, and that she had borne a child by him. Agrippa's colleague Maecenas points out that Antony must now give Cleopatra up for his future wife, Octavia, renowned for her modesty and virtue as well as her beauty. Enobarbus's response is immediate and unambiguous.

> *Maec.:* Now Antony must leave her utterly.
> *Eno.:* Never; he will not:
> Age cannot wither her, nor custom stale
> Her infinite variety: other women cloy
> The appetites they feed, but she makes hungry,
> Where most she satisfies.

The soothsayer warns Antony

It is evening, and Antony is bidding goodnight to Octavia and Caesar. He urges Octavia to trust him; he accepts that he has been wayward in the past, but promises that he will be a reliable and faithful husband to her.

As the others leave, Antony is joined by the soothsayer, who has accompanied him on his journey to Rome. The soothsayer is certain of one thing: Antony must keep his distance from Caesar. Despite Antony's courage and vigour, Caesar has an uncanny aura of good luck and success which will always unnerve and confound Antony when he is in Caesar's presence.

Antony does not want to hear, and orders the soothsayer to leave. However, he knows his comments to be true. The way that good fortune seems to be consistently on Caesar's side has always frustrated and bewildered him:

> *Antony:* The very dice obey him,
> And in our sports my better cunning faints*
> Under his chance...
>
> * *comes to nothing*

The soothsayer's words make Antony long more than ever to get back to the security, and pleasure, of Egypt.

The military response begins

Antony dispatches his general Ventidius to the eastern border of the Empire. He is to command an army whose mission is to drive out the invading Parthians.

The three Triumvirs leave Rome and lead their forces south, to Mount Misena, to confront the ambitious Pompey.

Bad news for Cleopatra

Cleopatra continues to while away the time, moody, impatient, unable to concentrate on anything but her thoughts and memories of Antony.

When a messenger arrives from Rome, she is so desperate to hear good news that she hardly gives him time to speak. She establishes that Antony is alive and well, but there is an uneasiness in the messenger's manner that makes her frantic with worry.

Finally the messenger breaks the news; Antony is married to Octavia. Cleopatra, distraught with rage, beats him mercilessly. She tries, unsuccessfully, to make him contradict himself. Eventually she pulls out a knife and the messenger runs out, proclaiming his innocence.

Cleopatra calms down a little, and calls the unwilling messenger back. She asks him yet again whether Antony is married, and receives the same answer. She dismisses him contemptuously. However, shortly after he has left, she sends an attendant after him; she is curious to know more about Octavia, and wants the messenger back yet again so that she can have a detailed description of her rival.

> *"How different, how very different from the home life of our own dear Queen!"*
>
> Comment by an elderly lady, supposedly overheard at a performance of *Antony and Cleopatra* in the 19th century, in the reign of Queen Victoria.

A deal is struck with Pompey

The three rulers of the Empire have come to meet Pompey face to face near his stronghold of Mount Misena. They have already let him know the peace terms they propose: that the territories of Sicily and Sardinia will be his if he calls off his rebellion, keeps the sea around Italy free of pirates, and provides regular shipments of wheat to Rome.

In an emotional speech, Pompey claims that his motive for invading Italy was to avenge the death of his father, who had ruled the Empire jointly with Julius Caesar many years before, and who had been defeated in civil war and murdered. His listeners are unmoved: all they want to know is whether Pompey accepts the terms offered. If not, they are ready to declare war.

Pompey hesitates. He brings up the subject of his father's house, which he claims Antony has appropriated, but again his listeners refuse to be distracted. Then he mentions the support and refuge that he gave to Antony's mother during the recent conflict in Rome, for which he has heard no word of thanks.

Antony assures Pompey that he is well aware of the debt of gratitude he owes him, and thanks him generously. This is enough to bring Pompey's hesitation to an end: he decides to accept the Triumvirate's terms.

A treaty of peace between the Triumvirate and Pompey is to be signed and sealed, and the event is to be celebrated with a series of feasts. The first will take place straight away on Pompey's galley, moored nearby, to which the leaders now make their way.

Enobarbus stays behind to talk with Menas, one of the pirates allied to Pompey. Menas is disillusioned; he had hoped that Pompey would refuse the offer of peace, and press on with his attack on the Empire.

The subject of Antony's marriage crops up, and Enobarbus once again predicts that Antony will return to Cleopatra and fall out with Caesar:

> *Eno.:* ... you shall find the band that seems to tie their
> friendship together will be the very strangler of their
> amity: Octavia is of a holy, cold and still conversation.*
> *Menas:* Who would not have his wife so?
> *Eno.:* Not he that himself is not so; which is Mark Antony. He
> will to his Egyptian dish again: then shall the sighs of
> Octavia blow the fire up in Caesar...
>
> ** character*

"Shakespeare opened his tragic career... with Romeo and Juliet, *and he closed it... with* Antony and Cleopatra. *These are both love tragedies, the one of youth, the other of maturity, and the fact that only twelve or thirteen years divide them shows the bitter rapidity of the maturing.*"

M. R. Ridley, Introduction to the Arden edition of *Antony and Cleopatra*, 1954

On board Pompey's galley, the drink is flowing freely.

The contrasts between the three leaders are highlighted by their differing reactions to drinking and feasting. Antony is in his element: he is animated and voluble, raring to descend into a boisterous, drunken oblivion. Caesar, austere and self-controlled, is uncomfortable with the effects of alcohol:

> *Caesar:* It's monstrous labour when I wash my brain
> And it grow fouler.
> *Antony:*   Be a child o' the time.
> *Caesar:* Possess it, I'll make answer...

Lepidus, in his anxiety to reconcile the two dominant characters, proposes one toast after another. He ignores his own lack of capacity for drink, and is reduced to an object of ridicule.

In the midst of all the noise and festivity, Menas manages to attract Pompey's attention, and takes him aside. He has a sober, sinister proposition: with Pompey's permission, he will cut the cable, put the galley out to sea and slaughter the three Roman leaders. Pompey can then become sole ruler of the Empire.

Pompey is thrown into confusion; he cannot, for the sake of his honour, agree to the plan, but at the same time he wishes that Menas had done it without his knowledge. To Menas's disgust, Pompey rejects his suggestion.

The drinking, dancing and music carry on, and the party becomes more and more riotous. Lepidus, unable to stay upright, is carried off. Caesar, increasingly uncomfortable with the general disorder, leaves early. Antony and Pompey go ashore to continue the party. Enobarbus and Menas stay on board to drink the rest of the night away.

Antony's lieutenant triumphs

III, i

Ventidius, sent by Antony to repel the invading Parthians in the east of the Empire, has routed the enemy. As his troops march through the Syrian desert, the body of Pacorus, son of the Parthian leader, is paraded before them in triumph.

Silius, a Roman officer, urges Ventidius to continue his offensive while they have the advantage, and occupy more territory for Antony and the Empire. Ventidius refuses: he knows that Antony would be displeased if a subordinate took too much of the limelight.

"Nowhere in the drama is the ridicule of worldly power more concentrated and effective than in the scene on Pompey's galley... It is the spirit of tragedy masquerading as farce, the chariot of comedy driven by death... Here Shakespeare is plainly paying his compliments to the fatuousness of a humanity that can delegate all its power to three drunken men on a boat - let its destiny depend on the slender string of a galley's cable and the still slenderer string of one weak man's 'honour'... "

Harold C. Goddard, *The Meaning of Shakespeare*, 1951

Antony and Octavia leave Rome

Antony and Octavia, now married, are about to set off for Antony's home in Athens. Caesar urges Antony to treat his sister well. There is a moment of suppressed tension between the two men as Antony becomes defensive about his role as a faithful husband:

> *Caesar:*   ... for better might we
> Have lov'd without this mean,* if on both parts
> This be not cherish'd.**
> *Antony:*   Make me not offended
> In your distrust.
> *Caesar:*   I have said.
> *Antony:*   You shall not find,
> Though you be therein curious, the least cause
> For what you seem to fear...
>
> ** this course of action (Antony's marriage to Octavia)*
> *** if we do not both cherish Octavia equally*

Caesar manages, with difficulty, to contain his sadness at Octavia's parting. Octavia is so full of emotion that she can hardly speak without crying: as Antony says, with great tenderness,

> *Antony:* Her tongue will not obey her heart, nor can
> Her heart inform her tongue - the swan's down feather,
> That stands upon the swell at the full of tide,
> And neither way inclines.

> *"In all these uneasy exchanges, the one element that remains pure is the capacity of Octavia to strike from those around her a redeeming note of poetry."*
>
> Derek Traversi, *Shakespeare: The Roman Plays*, 1963

More news for Cleopatra

The messenger who first brought Cleopatra news of Antony's marriage has returned, hesitant after his previous beating.

Cleopatra questions the messenger closely about Octavia's appearance and behaviour. She manages to find fault with every feature that he reports, except for her age, about which she remains silent: the messenger unwisely estimates Octavia's age as around thirty, several years younger than Cleopatra.

Overall, however, Cleopatra is reassured. She decides that Octavia does not pose a real threat to her relationship with Antony. She rewards the messenger with gold and the promise of further employment.

Antony loses patience with Caesar

The principal threats to the Empire have been dealt with, but relations between its two main rulers are far from settled.

Antony, now living in Athens with Octavia, is distrustful of Caesar, and is angered by his recent actions. Without consulting Antony, Caesar has been waging war against Pompey, despite their earlier treaty.

However, what has most enraged Antony is Caesar's reported slighting of him in public. Even if no actual insult was spoken, Antony, acutely aware of the importance of honour and reputation, believes that Caesar has been ungenerous when speaking of him:

Antony:
> ... when perforce he could not
> But pay me terms of honour,* cold and sickly
> He vented them; most narrow measure lent me:
> When the best hint was given him, he not took't,
> Or did it from his teeth.

> * *when he had no choice but to make favourable comments*

Octavia, torn between her love for her husband and her brother, is distraught. She realises that the consequences of conflict between the two leaders would be horrific:

Octavia:
> Wars 'twixt you twain would be
> As if the world should cleave, and that slain men
> Should solder up the rift.

The language of *Antony and Cleopatra* is densely packed with recurring images and themes. The word 'world', for example, is used far more frequently here than in any other play by Shakespeare.

"This single city, Rome, had conquered the world and produced a multitude of heroes... One is constantly aware that the stake in the struggle for domination is the whole world."

Allan Bloom, *Shakespeare's Politics*, 1964

Octavia intends to go to Caesar and act as a mediator between the two men. Antony grudgingly agrees to the visit, but warns her that he is preparing for war. His message is simple and blunt: she had better decide whose side she is on.

Caesar keeps a cool head   III, v - vi

Back in Rome, Caesar has been gaining ground relentlessly. He has defeated Pompey and retaken the territory previously granted to him. He has imprisoned Lepidus - having made use of his forces in the fight against Pompey - and dismissed him from the Triumvirate, confiscating all his wealth. Pompey, fleeing eastwards from Sicily, has been executed by Antony's officers.

Caesar is keeping a close eye on Antony's activities, and his spies have informed him that Antony is now in Egypt. Caesar hears, with disapproval, that Antony has been handing out territories to Cleopatra and her children in extravagant, gaudy ceremonies.

Caesar has received Antony's accusations that he has not shared out the territory regained from Pompey, and that he has unlawfully deposed Lepidus. His answer is already on the way. He is prepared to negotiate over Sicily, providing that Antony is ready to give Caesar a share of his conquests in the east. As for Lepidus, it was necessary to remove him from office; Caesar argues, without a hint of irony, that Lepidus had grown too cruel, and was abusing his position of authority.

Clearly, neither answer is going to satisfy Antony. Civil war has come a step closer.

Bad news for Octavia

While Caesar is in discussion with his generals about a suitable response to Antony, Octavia arrives.

She has come from Athens to try to heal the rift between the two leaders. Although authorised by Antony to spend as much as she wanted on her voyage, she has come quietly and without ceremony, much to Caesar's irritation:

> *Caesar:* Why have you stol'n upon us thus? You come not
> Like Caesar's sister: the wife of Antony
> Should have an army for an usher, and
> The neighs of horse to tell of her approach,
> Long ere she did appear.
>   ... you are come
> A market-maid to Rome, and have prevented
> The ostentation of our love; which, left unshown,
> Is often left unlov'd...

Caesar immediately pre-empts any peace-making attempt on Octavia's part. He asks her where Antony is now: she assumes he is at home in Athens, but Caesar informs her that, since her departure, Antony has slipped away to Egypt. Along with Cleopatra, he is preparing for war. He has already enlisted the help of dozens of kingdoms in Africa and the East.

Caesar reassures Octavia that the defeat of the adulterous Antony is necessary, inevitable and just. There is no point in her worrying about the impending war:

> *Caesar:* ... Be you not troubled with the time, which drives
> O'er your content these strong necessities,*
> But let determin'd things to destiny
> Hold unbewail'd their way.**
>
> *which forces these necessary events along,
> regardless of your happiness
> ** let predestined events take their course, without
> grieving

The unhappy Octavia has no choice but to give up Antony and stay in Rome with her brother.

> *"... Octavia seems to tell of another life than that of Alexandrian indulgence, a narrower life of obligations and pieties beside which the carnival of impulse is both glorified and condemned."*
>
> Mungo MacCallum, *Shakespeare's Roman plays and their background*, 1910

Caesar makes the first move

Antony is back with Cleopatra. The two of them are preparing for war with Caesar, and have set up a military camp at Actium on the west coast of Greece.

Enobarbus is trying to dissuade Cleopatra from taking part personally in the war, believing that she will distract Antony rather than help him. Cleopatra contradicts him angrily. While they are arguing, Antony enters. He has received news that Caesar's fleet has already set out from Italy, crossed the sea to Albania, and captured the coastal city of Toryne.

Antony's land army is strong, experienced and prepared; his sea forces, by contrast, are ill-equipped and unready. Despite this, he decides, impulsively, that he will fight Caesar at sea.

Antony's followers try desperately to dissuade him. They believe that Caesar's advance is designed to lure Antony out to sea, and that he should not respond to the challenge. But, precisely because he views Caesar's advance as a personal provocation, Antony is unable to resist the prospect of a sea-battle. Antony's own more grandiose challenge to Caesar - that they should settle their differences by single combat - has already been turned down.

Then Cleopatra intervenes. She offers Antony the use of her own fleet of sixty ships. Antony's mind is made up: any ships for which there are insufficient crews will be burned, the rest will be packed with men, and they will sail from Actium to confront Caesar at sea.

Caesar's gamble

The two navies and armies are lining up against one another at Actium.

Caesar does not know whether Antony has prepared to fight first at land or at sea. He instructs his lieutenant to keep his land forces out of action for the present; everything is to be staked on a sea-battle against the combined fleets of Antony and Cleopatra.

Cleopatra retreats; Antony follows

Caesar's gamble pays off. In the midst of the sea-battle, when neither side has the upper hand, Cleopatra leads her sixty galleys away from the fight, creating utter confusion and demoralisation. To make matters worse, Antony, in his fleet's flagship, sails after her.

On a hillside overlooking the sea-battle, Scarus, one of Antony's foot-soldiers, watches with horror and disbelief:

> *Scarus:*   ... we have kiss'd away
>   Kingdoms, and provinces.
> *Eno.:*   How appears the fight?
> *Scarus:* On our side, like the token'd pestilence,*
>   Where death is sure.
>
>   * *the first appearance of the plague, when infection*
>   *is shown by red blotches on the skin*

Some of Antony's followers are already deserting to Caesar's camp. Enobarbus knows that he ought to do the same, but decides to stick with Antony.

The lovers are reunited

Now back in Egypt, Antony has sunk into a state of despair and self-hatred. He offers his remaining followers gold and letters of safe conduct so that they can make their way to Caesar's ranks.

For the time being Antony wishes to be left alone, to reflect on the dishonour of his present situation and the glories of his past. He is starting to feel old.

Cleopatra enters. She is unwilling to approach Antony, and is barely able to speak, except to ask Antony's forgiveness; she had not expected him to follow her in retreat. Antony responds passionately:

> *Antony:* Egypt, thou knew'st too well,
> My heart was to thy rudder tied by the strings,
> And thou shouldst tow me after.

Antony has already sent an ambassador to Caesar, and is grimly contemplating the prospect of surrender to the younger man. However, Cleopatra's tears finally rouse him out of his weary resignation. As he forgives her, and comforts her, his fighting spirit starts to return:

> *Antony:* Fall not a tear, I say, one of them rates
> All that is won and lost...
>   ... Fortune knows,
> We scorn her most, when most she offers blows.

Caesar states his terms

Caesar's forces have pursued Antony and Cleopatra to Alexandria, and are now camped outside the city. Antony's ambassador arrives to speak to Caesar.

The man Antony has sent is his children's schoolmaster. Caesar's followers see this as a significant choice; the kings and warlords who had previously served Antony have all deserted him. The request made by the defeated Antony is simple and modest: he wishes to be allowed to live in Egypt - or, failing that, in Athens - as a private citizen. As for Cleopatra, she asks that Egypt should stay in the hands of her descendants.

Caesar's response is immediate. He rejects Antony's request out of hand. He is prepared to listen to Cleopatra, and treat her sympathetically, on the condition that she delivers Antony up to Caesar - or executes him herself.

After the schoolmaster has left, Caesar sends his own envoy, Thidias, to Cleopatra. His mission is to win her over from Antony's influence. He has Caesar's authority to make as many promises - or bribes - as necessary.

> *"Brevity, energy and firmness of decision are the qualities which, advancing remorselessly upon Antony, will effect his ruin."*
>
> Derek Traversi, *Shakespeare: The Roman Plays*, 1963

35

Antony issues a challenge

Antony is told of Caesar's demands. He announces the news, bluntly, to Cleopatra:

Antony: To the boy Caesar send this grizzled* head,
And he will fill thy wishes to the brim,
With principalities.

* *greying*

Aggrieved by the success of the youthful Caesar, Antony is becoming increasingly irrational. He decides once again to challenge Caesar to single combat, the two of them to be armed only with swords. He leaves, along with the schoolmaster, to compose a suitable message for dispatch to Caesar.

Enobarbus, still loyal to Antony, is dismayed: the idea that Caesar will risk everything in a sword-fight with Antony is laughable. He can see that Antony's grasp on reality is slipping:

Eno.:   ... Caesar, thou hast subdued
His judgment too.

"The heroes are restless, like big animals in a cage. The cage gets smaller and smaller, and they writhe more and more violently."

Jan Kott, *Shakespeare Our Contemporary*, 1965

Caesar's messenger is whipped

While Antony is preparing his challenge, Caesar's messenger Thidias arrives. He treats Cleopatra with reassurance and courtesy. Caesar pities her, he explains, for her unwilling submission to Antony, whom she clearly does not love. She should now take the opportunity to reject Antony and put herself under Caesar's protection.

Cleopatra decides to play along with this line of argument, and says that she will gladly throw herself on Caesar's mercy. To confirm her surrender, she allows Thidias to kiss her hand.

At this point, Antony returns. He flies into a rage, denouncing Cleopatra as a whore, and calls for the messenger to be whipped mercilessly. When his servants are slow to respond, he becomes even more furious:

> *Antony:*   Now, gods and devils,
> Authority melts from me: of late, when I cried 'Ho!'
> Like boys unto a muss,* kings would start forth,
> And cry 'Your will?' Have you no ears?
> I am Antony yet.**
>
> * *scramble*
> ** *still*

Thidias is whipped violently and sent back to Caesar. Antony does not care about the consequences: he wants to shake Caesar, to make him realise how how angry he is. As far as he is concerned, Caesar can get his own back by whipping Antony's messenger - or even hanging him.

Antony decides to fight it out

Antony continues to rage against Cleopatra for her familiarity with a follower of Caesar's. Finally, Cleopatra manages to convince him that her love for him is absolutely unwavering.

Antony's anger subsides, but the episode has roused him into a state of passion and recklessness. Rather than surrender to Caesar, or meet him in single combat, he now decides to gather all his remaining troops and attack Caesar's camp in a full-scale battle.

With Cleopatra's encouragement, he becomes excited at the prospect of being in the thick of battle again. Tonight, he orders, there will be feasting:

> *Antony:*   ... I'll set my teeth,
> And send to darkness all that stop me. Come,
> Let's have one other gaudy* night: call to me
> All my sad captains, fill our bowls once more;
> Let's mock the midnight bell.
>
> * *wild, festive*

Enobarbus does not share the general excitement. As far as he is concerned, Antony has now deluded himself into believing that he is invincible. Enobarbus decides that he has had enough. It is time to leave Antony.

Caesar plans his final move

News of Antony's erratic, violent behaviour reaches Caesar's camp, where it is seen as a good sign. His fortunes are clearly at a low ebb, and, as Maecenas says, it is time to go in for the kill:

> *Maec.:* ... When one so great begins to rage, he's hunted
> Even to falling.

Caesar plans to attack the next day. He is confident of an easy victory; many of Antony's followers have by now deserted him, and his army is greatly reduced.

Emotions run high in Antony's camp

News arrives at Cleopatra's palace that Caesar has refused Antony's offer of single combat. Antony hears the message with resignation. Only one course of action now remains open: tomorrow he and his remaining followers must fight to the death, at land and sea, against the full force of Caesar's assembled troops.

Antony becomes sentimental as he thanks his followers for their loyalty. Many of them are reduced to tears, sensing that he is preparing to leave them forever. However, Antony's mood changes suddenly, and he insists that it is victory, not death, that is in his thoughts. Finally, he invites everyone to join him in a bout of feasting and drinking to end all this painful contemplation:

> *Antony:*　　　　　　　Let's to supper, come,
> And drown consideration.

An omen

It is the night before the battle. The soldiers guarding Cleopatra's palace hear strange music all around them. It seems to be coming from under the ground, but they cannot track down its source.

The soldiers are shaken. They take this as a sign that the spirit of Hercules, the god that Antony worships, is leaving him.

The historical Marcus Antonius, like Shakespeare's character, claimed to be descended from Hercules. This is how the Greek historian Plutarch, who lived in the century after Antony, describes him:

"... Now it had been a speeche of old time, that the familie of the Antonii were discended from one Anton, the sonne of Hercules, whereof the familie tooke name. This opinion did Antonius seeke to confirme in all his doings: not onely resembling him in the likenes of his body, but also in the wearing of his garments. For when he would openly shewe him selfe abroad before many people, he would alwayes weare his cassocke gyrt downe lowe upon his hippes, with a great sword hanging by his side, and upon that, some ill favored cloke... things that seeme intollerable in other men, as to boast commonly, to jeast with one or other, to drinke like a good fellow with every body, to sit with the souldiers when they dine, and to eate and drinke with them souldierlike: it is incredible what wonderfull love it wanne him amongest them."

Plutarch, *Lives of the Noble Grecians and Romans*, translated by Sir Thomas North, 1579

If they are right, the soothsayer's earlier judgement, warning Antony to stay away from Caesar, has proved true:

> *Sooth.:* ... Thy demon, that thy spirit which keeps thee, is
> Noble, courageous, high, unmatchable,
> Where Caesar's is not. But near him, thy angel
> Becomes afeard...

Antony prepares for battle   IV, iv - v

On the morning of the battle, Antony is up early. He is cheerful, confident, and raring for action. Cleopatra is determined to help him on with his armour, and Antony tolerates her inexperienced efforts with good humour and pride.

Antony is not the only one up early. Many of his soldiers are already prepared and armoured, ahead of time, and a sense of hope and excitement is in the air.

As Antony is greeting his troops, he hears some unwelcome news: Enobarbus has deserted him. The news causes Antony a moment's sadness, but he is not bitter. Blaming himself rather than Enobarbus, he orders that Enobarbus's possessions and wealth should be carefully gathered together and sent after him. A letter bidding him farewell and wishing him success is also to be sent; Antony will sign it himself.

Caesar looks forward to a time of peace

Caesar directs his general Agrippa to start the attack. Unlike Antony, he will not be present on the battlefield himself.

While Antony is fighting as a matter of personal honour, and out of a sheer love of battle, Caesar is motivated by a broader sense of purpose. Victory will not only give him sole control of the Empire; it will finally bring an end to civil war and internal division.

> *Caesar:* The time of universal peace is near:
> Prove this a prosperous day, the three-nook'd* world
> Shall bear the olive** freely.
>
> * *three-cornered: made up of land, sea and sky*
> ** *olive branch, symbol of peace*

Although Caesar's ultimate vision may be one of peace and stability, he is ruthless and unsentimental in his means of achieving it. He decides to use the deserters from Antony's army in the forefront of his own attack:

> *Caesar:* ... Plant those that have revolted in the vant,*
> That** Antony may seem to spend his fury
> Upon himself.
>
> * *vanguard, front line*
> ** *so that*

Enobarbus, now in Caesar's camp, reflects ruefully on his decision to leave Antony. When he learns of Antony's generous, forgiving gesture he is overcome with regret and shame.

The time of universal peace is near...

There is a profound unconscious significance in Caesar's words which would have been immediately apparent to an audience of Shakespeare's time. Although Caesar has in mind the end of civil strife within the Empire, to Christians - followers of the Prince of Peace - his words also carry spiritual overtones.

Octavius Caesar was later to become the Emperor Augustus, sole ruler of Rome, a title which he held for over forty years until his death in 14 A.D. It was during his rule that, in an eastern province of the Roman Empire, the event considered by Christians to be the turning point of history occurred:

"And it came to pass in those days, that there went out a decree from Caesar Augustus, that all the world should be taxed. And all went to be taxed, every one into his own city. And Joseph also went up from Galilee, out of the city of Nazareth, into Judaea, unto the city of David, which is called Bethlehem; to be taxed with Mary his espoused wife, being great with child... And she brought forth her first-born son, and wrapped him in swaddling clothes, and laid him in a manger; because there was no room for them at the inn."

Gospel According To St. Luke, *King James Bible*, 1611

Antony gains the upper hand

Against all the odds, the sheer ferocity and determination of Antony's army is proving too much for Caesar's forces.

In their impassioned fury, Antony's soldiers have made such inroads that the unthinkable has happened: the turmoil of battle is threatening to shake the orderly, planned surroundings of Caesar himself. Agrippa is forced to order a retreat:

> *Agr.:*   Retire, we have engag'd ourselves too far:
> Caesar himself has work...

Returning from the battle, Antony is in high spirits, his vigour restored by the day's fighting. He enthusiastically proclaims his praise for his soldiers, his devotion to Cleopatra and his eager anticipation of tomorrow's fighting.

> *"The world is varied and multifarious, but the world is small. Too small for three rulers. Too small even for two. Either Antony, or Caesar, must die. Antony and Cleopatra is a tragedy about the smallness of the world."*
>
> Jan Kott, *Shakespeare Our Contemporary*, 1965

Enobarbus dies of remorse

A group of Caesar's soldiers, on guard outside his camp, overhear a man's voice. They go to investigate. It is Enobarbus, wandering alone in the humid night air.

Tormented beyond endurance by his own feelings of regret, he has lost the will to go on. He wishes only to express his repentance, and then to die. He calls on the moon to hear his prayer and bring his suffering to an end:

> *Eno.:*   O sovereign mistress of true melancholy...
>   ... Throw my heart
> Against the flint and hardness of my fault,
> Which being dried with grief, will break to powder,
> And finish all foul thoughts.

His prayer is answered. He collapses, and with his dying breath asks Antony's forgiveness. Caesar's soldiers carry him away.

An easy victory

The day after the disastrous land-battle, Caesar launches an attack on the combined naval forces of Antony and Cleopatra.

Antony remains on land with his army. At its head is Scarus, who fought heroically in the previous day's action against Caesar. Although he does not tell Antony, Scarus is pessimistic about their prospects at sea. He has heard about the appearance of an unlucky sign:

> *Scarus:*   Swallows have built
> In Cleopatra's sails their nests. The augurers*
> Say, they know not, they cannot tell, look grimly,
> And dare not speak their knowledge.
>
> * *soothsayers*

Antony watches the sea-battle from a hillside. To his horror, the fleet appears to offer no resistance: the crews even join those in Caesar's ships and start celebrating. Caesar has finally won.

Antony, convinced that Cleopatra has come to a secret agreement with Caesar, is enraged. He orders Scarus to dismiss all his troops; the war is over, and his only aim now is vengeance against Cleopatra.

At this moment Cleopatra herself, unaware of what has happened, comes to meet Antony. Hardly able to contain himself, he orders her to leave before he takes her life. Caesar will have her dragged through the streets of Rome as a trophy, he tells her scornfully as she runs away:

> *Antony:* Vanish, or I shall give thee thy deserving,
> And blemish Caesar's triumph. Let him take thee,
> And hoist thee up to the shouting plebeians...
> .. let
> Patient Octavia plough thy visage up
> With her prepared nails.

As soon as Cleopatra has gone, Antony regrets having allowed her to escape alive. Burning with anger and desire for revenge, he decides that Cleopatra must die.

Cleopatra takes refuge in the monument IV, xiii

Fearing for her life, Cleopatra retreats to her monument, a tall, fortified building intended to serve as her future tomb. She takes her two servants and companions, Charmian and Iras, with her.

In an attempt to calm Antony's rage, she instructs another attendant, Mardian, to tell Antony that she is dead:

> *Cleo.:* Mardian, go tell him I have slain myself:
> Say, that the last I spoke was 'Antony,'
> And word it, prithee, piteously.

Antony reaches the end

Antony, his temper now subsided, is reflecting on his downfall in the company of Eros, his last loyal companion.

Antony's power, authority and reputation have all disappeared, leaving him lost and empty. Cleopatra's love for him, which he had thought was constant, has slipped away too, and his life has no more substance than a drifting cloud:

> *Antony:* Sometime we see a cloud that's dragonish,
> A vapour sometime, like a bear, or lion,
> A tower'd citadel, a pendent rock,
> A forked mountain, or blue promontory
> With trees upon 't, that nod unto the world,
> And mock our eyes with air...
> That which is now a horse, even with a thought
> The rack dislimns,* and makes it indistinct
> As water is in water...
> My good knave Eros, now thy captain is
> Even such a body: here I am Antony,
> Yet cannot hold this visible shape...
>
> ** the shifting clouds cause the image to disintegrate*

Now that Cleopatra has deserted him for Caesar, there is no reason to go on living.

> *"Antony's fallen state is represented most brilliantly by the imagery of dissolution. The pattern in the play is one of melting, fading, dissolving... and losing of form that marks his downward course after Actium."*
>
> Maurice Charney, *Shakespeare's Roman Plays*, 1961

The arrival of Mardian briefly rouses Antony's anger again as he is reminded of Cleopatra's treachery. However, the news he brings - that Cleopatra has died by her own hand - leaves Antony stunned and desolate.

> *Antony:* Unarm, Eros, the long day's task is done,
> And we must sleep.

Antony sadly takes off his battered armour and prepares for death. He calls to the spirit of the dead Cleopatra, now forgiven, telling her that he will be with her soon:

> *Antony:*   ... Stay for me,
> Where souls do couch* on flowers, we'll hand in hand,
> And with our sprightly port** make the ghosts gaze...
>
> * *lie down, rest*
> ** *exuberance, vitality*

In the past, Antony has made Eros swear that, when the time came, he would take Antony's life rather than let him face humiliation at the hands of Caesar. That time has now come; Antony tells Eros to keep his promise and kill him.

At first, Eros cannot bring himself to obey, despite Antony's impatient urging. He finally agrees, on the condition that Antony turns away from him. When Antony's back is turned, Eros draws his sword and slays himself.

Antony realises that this is the honourable thing to do. He runs himself through with his sword.

Cleopatra's message arrives too late

Antony is fatally wounded, but not dead. Lacking the strength to finish the task, he calls out for his guards and implores them to kill him. They refuse, and flee in terror.

However, one of Antony's followers, Decretas, realises that there is something to be gained from the situation. If he is the first to break the news to Caesar, he decides, he is likely to be treated leniently. He hurries off to Caesar's camp, taking as proof the sword that Antony has just used.

One of Cleopatra's attendants now arrives. Cleopatra is not dead, he tells Antony: it was his suspicion that she had negotiated with Caesar, and his rage, that drove her to deceive him. He assures Antony, emphatically, that Cleopatra has not had any dealings at all with Caesar.

Antony asks his last few followers and guards to perform a final service for him; to carry him to the monument to be with Cleopatra.

> "Antony's method of suicide, the ancient Roman custom of running on his sword, is like the earlier impulse to single combat, a heroic gesture which belongs to another time. For Antony's personal dream is a kind of myth-making, the translation of the mortal to the immortal."
>
> Marjorie B. Garber, *Dream in Shakespeare: from Metaphor to Metamorphosis*, 1974

Antony and Cleopatra reunited

Cleopatra, sombre and resigned, waits in her monument. She is fearful for Antony's safety; at the same time, she has a premonition that her own life is nearing its end.

Antony, by now near death, is brought to the foot of the monument. He asks Cleopatra for one final kiss:

> *Antony:* I am dying, Egypt, dying; only
> I here importune death* awhile, until
> Of many thousand kisses, the poor last
> I lay upon thy lips.
>
> ** ask death to wait*

Cleopatra cannot come down from her stronghold for fear of being captured: instead, Antony is hauled painfully up into the monument for a last embrace. He urges Cleopatra to make an honourable peace with Caesar, and asks to be remembered as a noble, courageous Roman. His fortunes, sinking for so long, reach their final depths, and he dies.

> *Cleo.:*   O, see, my women:
> The crown o' the earth doth melt.

Cleopatra faints; for a moment it seems that she too has died. But she recovers, and becomes calm, almost cheerful. The world without Antony is not worth living in, so the prospect of death is to be welcomed. Suicide, favoured by the Romans in defeat, will be both an honour and an adventure:

> *Cleo.:*   ... what's brave, what's noble,
> Let's do it after the high Roman fashion,
> And make death proud to take us.

Caesar is shaken

Decretas, who took the dying Antony's sword, arrives in Caesar's camp and breaks the news.

Caesar's first reaction is disbelief and shock. The departure of such a powerful spirit should have made the earth itself tremble:

> *Caesar:* The breaking of so great a thing should make
> A greater crack. The round world
> Should have shook lions into civil streets,*
> And citizens to their dens.
>
> * *orderly city streets*

As the news sinks in, Caesar is moved to tears. He does not regret the war he has waged against Antony, knowing it to have been necessary: nevertheless, he and his followers are sad that such a generous spirit should have to be sacrificed in the cause of the Empire.

"In the last two acts of Antony and Cleopatra *Shakespeare wrote as never before or after. To see them performed with a majesty equal to their mighty utterance of desire, ecstasy, despair, and the brave end has been my life's desire in the theatre, and now I have seen it done."*

Ivor Brown, writing in *The Observer*, 1951, on a performance with Laurence Olivier as Antony and Vivien Leigh as Cleopatra.

Caesar's intentions towards Cleopatra

A messenger arrives from Cleopatra, asking Caesar what he means to do with her in defeat. Caesar assures the messenger that Cleopatra will be treated with respect and kindness.

Once the messenger has left, a different picture emerges. Caesar is anxious that Cleopatra should be taken alive; however, it is his own glory, not Cleopatra's well-being, that he has in mind. She will be an invaluable prize in his triumphal celebrations back in Rome:

> *Caesar:*   ... her life in Rome
>   Would be eternal in our triumph...

Caesar sends some of his officers to negotiate with Cleopatra. They may promise her anything to prevent her from taking her own life, and to ensure her safe capture.

Cleopatra is seized   V, ii

Locked in her monument, with her faithful maidservants, Cleopatra muses on the simple, decisive, final act of suicide. Living, by contrast, has come to seem arduous, unpredictable and worthless.

Proculeius, one of Caesar's officers, arrives at the monument. He addresses Cleopatra courteously, explaining that Caesar is anxious to help her, not to punish her. She is invited to say what she requires of Caesar.

Cleopatra has only one request: that the kingdom of Egypt, now conquered by Caesar, should be inherited by her children. Proculeius assures her that Caesar will consider any request sympathetically.

While they are talking, a group of soldiers, headed by another of Caesar's officers, storms into the monument. Cleopatra draws a dagger and tries to stab herself, but she is seized and disarmed.

Robbed of the chance to take her life, Cleopatra flies into a frenzy of anger and despair. She is convinced that her fate, if she lives, is to be dragged around Rome in public humiliation. If she cannot take her own life, she warns, she will attempt to starve herself to death. Any fate will be preferable to being a living trophy of Caesar's:

> Cleo.: This mortal house I'll ruin,
> Do Caesar what he can. Know, sir, that I
> Will not wait pinion'd* at your master's court,
> Nor once be chastis'd with the sober eye
> Of dull Octavia.
> ... Rather a ditch in Egypt
> Be gentle grave unto me, rather on Nilus' mud
> Lay me stark-nak'd, and let the water-flies
> Blow me into abhorring...**
>
> * confined, like a bird with its wings clipped
> ** consume my body until it rots

Cleopatra's mind is made up. There is no choice now but death: all she needs is the means to achieve it.

> "Of all Shakespeare's historical plays, Antony and Cleopatra is by far the most wonderful... the fiery force is sustained throughout."
>
> Samuel Taylor Coleridge, Lectures, 1818

Antony remembered

Another Roman, Dolabella, takes over from Proculeius as Cleopatra's guard. He listens as Cleopatra, now calm and dreamy, summons up a majestic image of Antony:

Cleo.:   His legs bestrid the ocean, his rear'd arm
         Crested the world:* his voice was propertied
         As all the tuned spheres...**
                 ... For his bounty,
         There was no winter in 't: an autumn 'twas
         That grew the more by reaping: his delights
         Were dolphin-like, they show'd his back above
         The element they lived in...***

         * was raised over the whole world, like a heraldic
           symbol of domination and protection
         ** as beautiful as music generated by the revolving
           heavens
         *** he loved his pleasures, but his greatness was
           never submerged by them

Dolabella is touched by Cleopatra's plight. When she asks about Caesar's plans for her, he is unable to hide the truth. Whatever Caesar may say, his real intention is to take Cleopatra back to Rome and display her in a triumphal procession.

Caesar is deceived

Caesar himself, with his generals and attendants, now comes into the monument. His show of warmth and forgiveness towards Cleopatra is coupled with a dark hint as to the fate of her children if she should take her own life. Cleopatra plays along with Caesar's apparent benevolence, behaving in a suitably humble and apologetic way.

As Caesar is about to leave, a strange scene takes place, presumably planned in advance by Cleopatra. She hands Caesar a list of her possessions, declaring that, as victor, everything is his to dispose of as he sees fit. She calls on Seleucus, her treasurer, to confirm that it is a true account of her wealth.

With a great show of reluctance, Seleucus states that Cleopatra has left out at least half her riches from the list. Caesar is not shocked in the slightest; in fact he has difficulty in hiding his amusement.

Cleopatra puts on a convincing display of fury and embarrassment at this public indignity. The things she has failed to include in the list, she explains to Caesar, are mostly worthless articles. She has deliberately omitted a few valuable items: these were things that she wanted to keep so that she could later present them as gifts to Caesar's wife Livia and his sister Octavia.

Caesar diplomatically asks the treasurer to leave. He emphasises again that he does not intend to take anything from Cleopatra, and that his only concern is her comfort and well-being. When Cleopatra finally calms down, Caesar leaves, reassured that suicide is clearly the last thing on her mind.

However, as soon as Caesar has gone, it becomes clear that Cleopatra's only wish is to die; the scene with her treasurer was designed to fool Caesar into relaxing his guard over her. Cleopatra's attendants, Charmian and Iras, are united with her in her aim:

> Iras: Finish, good lady, the bright day is done,
>   And we are for the dark.

Dolabella returns surreptitiously for a brief visit. He brings news that Caesar plans to send Cleopatra and her children to Rome in the next few days. Cleopatra is determined to die rather than face humiliation. She conjures up a vivid picture of the public ridicule awaiting her in Rome, and imagines street performers putting on Egyptian sideshows:

> Cleo.:   The quick comedians
>   Extemporally will stage us, and present
>   Our Alexandrian revels: Antony
>   Shall be brought drunken forth, and I shall see
>   Some squeaking Cleopatra boy my greatness*
>   I' the posture of a whore.
>
> * *make an attempt to imitate my greatness, even*
>   *though the actor will be a mere boy*

It has been suggested that *Antony and Cleopatra* was not performed in Shakespeare's lifetime, as the part of Cleopatra was beyond the scope of the boy actors of the time. (It was to be another fifty years before actresses took part in public performances.) This is extremely unlikely: Shakespeare's major characters were usually created with particular members of his acting company in mind, and it is likely that the part of Cleopatra was created for a boy with a talent for playing powerful, ruthless women - in all probability the same boy who had already played Goneril (in *King Lear*) and Lady Macbeth.

The last visitor

Cleopatra sends her attendants out to bring her crown and robes. She remembers an earlier journey, when she sailed majestically along the river Cydnus, in her barge of gold and purple, to meet Antony for the first time: her voyage to the next world, to be reunited with Antony, is to be equally regal and stately.

A visitor, sent for by Cleopatra a few minutes ago, now arrives. He is a comical, talkative country bumpkin, bringing a basket of figs for the queen. The soldiers guarding Cleopatra let him enter the monument, thinking him harmless.

Hidden under the figs is a nest of asps, little snakes whose bite causes a quick, painless death. Cleopatra listens patiently as the simpleton, in his roundabout way, warns her of the danger of the snakes. As he leaves, Charmian and Iras return with Cleopatra's royal attire.

It was widely believed in Shakespeare's time that insects, snakes and other living creatures could be generated out of inanimate mud - such as that of the overflowing Nile - by the intense heat of the sun.

"The entrance of the clown juxtaposes the fruitful and death-dealing powers of the Nile: the figs and asps are both products of the same fertility."

Maurice Charney, *Shakespeare's Roman Plays*, 1961

> "... in the splendid poetic gesture of her final suicide, Cleopatra is redeemed at last into tragedy. She finds true pride, and dignity, and the quiet humor that sees over the other side of death without panic or self-pity. Yet she does not lose her original character. Her dying speech is as sensual as all her other speeches..."
>
> David Daiches, *A Critical History of English Literature*, 1960

Cleopatra joins Antony

Cleopatra's fortunes have sunk to their lowest ebb, as did Antony's earlier, under Caesar's relentless domination. Her spirit, though, is in the ascendant:

Cleo.: Give me my robe, put on my crown, I have
Immortal longings in me. Now no more
The juice of Egypt's grape shall moist this lip.
... I am fire, and air; my other elements
I give to baser life.

Kissing Cleopatra farewell, Iras falls and dies, overcome with grief. Cleopatra, passionately jealous to the last, fears that Iras will have the first kiss from Antony in the next world. She applies an asp to her breast and impatiently goads it into biting her.

As the life flows painlessly out of her, she comforts the distraught Charmian:

Char.: O eastern star!
Cleo.: Peace, peace!
Dost thou not see my baby at my breast,
That sucks the nurse asleep?
Char.: O, break! O, break!
Cleo.: As sweet as balm, as soft as air, as gentle.

Caesar pays his respects

Charmian closes Cleopatra's eyes and straightens her crown. As the soothsayer predicted so long ago, she has outlived her mistress. However, it is not to be for long. When the guards rush in, suspecting that something is wrong, she picks up an asp. By the time they realise what has happened, and call for Dolabella and Caesar, she too is dead.

Finding that he has failed to capture Cleopatra alive, Caesar reacts with admiration rather than anger. He cannot help gazing at her for a few moments, fascinated by the calm resolution showing in her face:

> *Caesar:*   ... she looks like sleep,
> As she would catch another Antony
> In her strong toil* of grace.
>
> * *labour: also, a net or snare*

"When Antony and Cleopatra kill themselves, the tragedy is over, but history and the world go on existing. The funeral oration over the corpses of Antony and Cleopatra is spoken by the victorious Triumvir, Octavius, the future Augustus Caesar... He is still talking, but the stage is empty. All the great ones have gone. And the world has become flat."

Jan Kott, *Shakespeare Our Contemporary*, 1965

Caesar reveals that he has spoken to Cleopatra's own physician, who told him that she has always shown an intense interest in the various ways of achieving a painless death. He orders his soldiers to carry the bodies away.

Caesar: Take up her bed,
        And bear her women from the monument;
        She shall be buried by her Antony.
        No grave upon the earth shall clip* in it
        A pair so famous...
                            Our army shall
        In solemn show attend this funeral,
        And then to Rome.

    * *clasp, embrace*

Caesar feels compassion, but no regret. Antony and Cleopatra have died: the Empire moves on.

———

Acknowledgements

The following publications have proved invaluable as sources of factual information and critical insight:

-   Allan Bloom, *Shakespeare's Politics*, Basic Books, 1964

-   John Russell Brown, *Antony and Cleopatra: A Casebook*, Macmillan, 1968

-   Charles Boyce, *Shakespeare A to Z*, Roundtable Press, 1990

-   Maurice Charney, *Shakespeare's Roman Plays*, Oxford University Press, 1961

-   David Daiches, *A Critical History of English Literature*, Secker and Warburg, 1960

-   Northrop Frye, *On Shakespeare*, Yale University Press, 1986

-   Marjorie B. Garber, *Dream in Shakespeare: from Metaphor to Metamorphosis*, Yale University Press, 1974

-   Harold C. Goddard, *The Meaning of Shakespeare*, University of Chicago Press, 1951

-   G. B. Harrison, *Introducing Shakespeare*, Pelican, 1966

-   Jan Kott, *Shakespeare Our Contemporary*, Doubleday, 1965

-   Mungo MacCallum, *Shakespeare's Roman plays and their background*, Macmillan, 1910

-   M. R. Ridley, Introduction to the Arden edition of *Antony and Cleopatra*, Methuen, 1954

-   Caroline Spurgeon, *Shakespeare's Imagery And What It Tells Us*, Cambridge University Press, 1935

-   Derek Traversi, *Shakespeare: The Roman Plays*, Hollis & Carter, 1963

-   John Wain, *The Living World of Shakespeare: A Playgoer's Guide*, Macmillan, 1964

All quotations from *Antony and Cleopatra* are taken from the Arden Shakespeare.

You can order the Shakespeare Handbooks direct from the publisher. Cut out this page - or make a photocopy - and send the completed form, together with a cheque or postal order, to:

Upstart Crow Publications
11, St John's Terrace
Lewes, East Sussex
BN7 2DL

		Number:	Cost:
Antony & Cleopatra ISBN 1 899747 02 8	£2.99		£
As You Like It ISBN 1 899747 00 1	£2.99		£
King Lear ISBN 1 899747 03 6	£3.99		£
Twelfth Night ISBN 1 899747 01 X	£2.99		£
Please add 40p postage & packing per book (maximum £2)			£
	Total:		£

Name:

Address:

Postcode:

Please make cheques / postal orders payable to **Upstart Crow Publications**.

If you would like to be informed when new titles in the
Shakespeare Handbooks series become available, tick here:

Upstart Crow Publications will not pass your address on to other organisations.

Prices correct at time of going to press. Whilst every effort is made to keep prices low, Upstart Crow Publications reserves the right to show new retail prices on covers which differ from those previously advertised in the text or elsewhere.